WEIRDO 10

MESSY WEIRD!

Scholastic Press
An imprint of Scholastic Australia Pty Limited (ABN 11 000 614 577)
PO Box 579 Gosford NSW 2250
www.scholastic.com.au

Part of the Scholastic Group
Sydney • Auckland • New York • Toronto • London • Mexico City
• New Delhi • Hong Kong • Buenos Aires • Puerto Rico

First published by Scholastic Australia in 2018.

NATIONAL LIBRARY OF AUSTRALIA

A catalogue record for this book is available from the National Library of Australia

ISBN: 978-93-5471-822-9

Typeset in Grenadine MVB, Push Ups and Lunch Box.

This reprint edition: February, 2025

Printed in India at Polykam offset New Delhi 110028

BLAH, BLAH, BLAH

ANH DO

Illustrated by JULES FABER

WEIRDO 10
MESSY WEIRD!

A SCHOLASTIC PRESS BOOK
FROM SCHOLASTIC AUSTRALIA

DING!

CHAPTER 1

We've just moved into our new house and it's **awesome!** The yard is like a **jungle!**

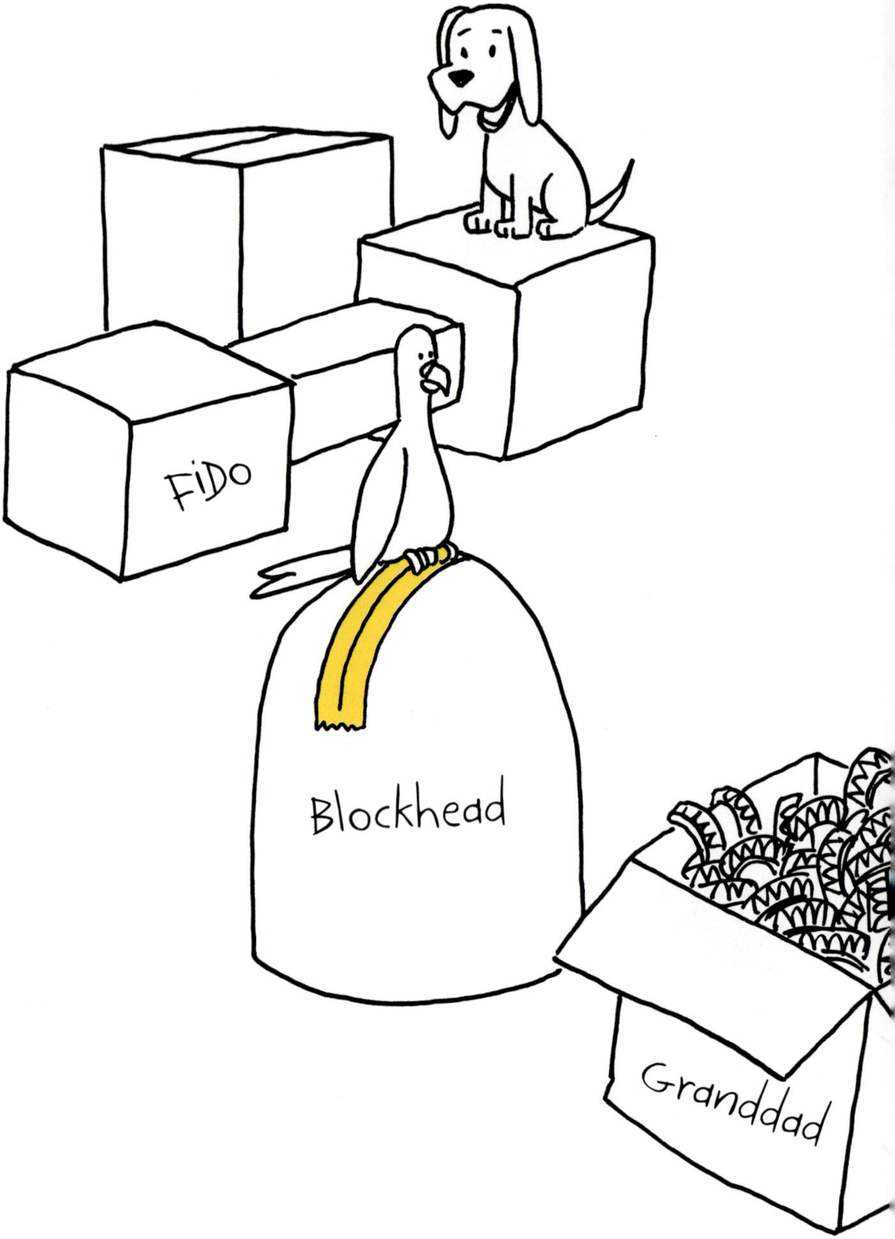
FIDO
Blockhead
Granddad

We still have **HEAPS** of unpacking to do . . .
there are **so**

many

boxes!

And there's LOADS of cleaning up

...everything's messy!

AND THESE
BLACK SQUARES
ARE ACTUALLY
WINDOWS!

But we're getting there . . . sort of . . . when we're not wasting time **MUCKING AROUND!**

Like Roger, who's been having heaps of fun **hiding** in our empty boxes . . .

. . . then giving us a **fright!**

FiDo and Blockhead found something really funny to do with all of our **bubble wrap** . . .

While unpacking, I keep finding funny things that I haven't seen in ages!

Like a bunch of old fold-ins I'd drawn!

A
Frilled-neck lizard

B Fold line B over to meet line A

sausage dog

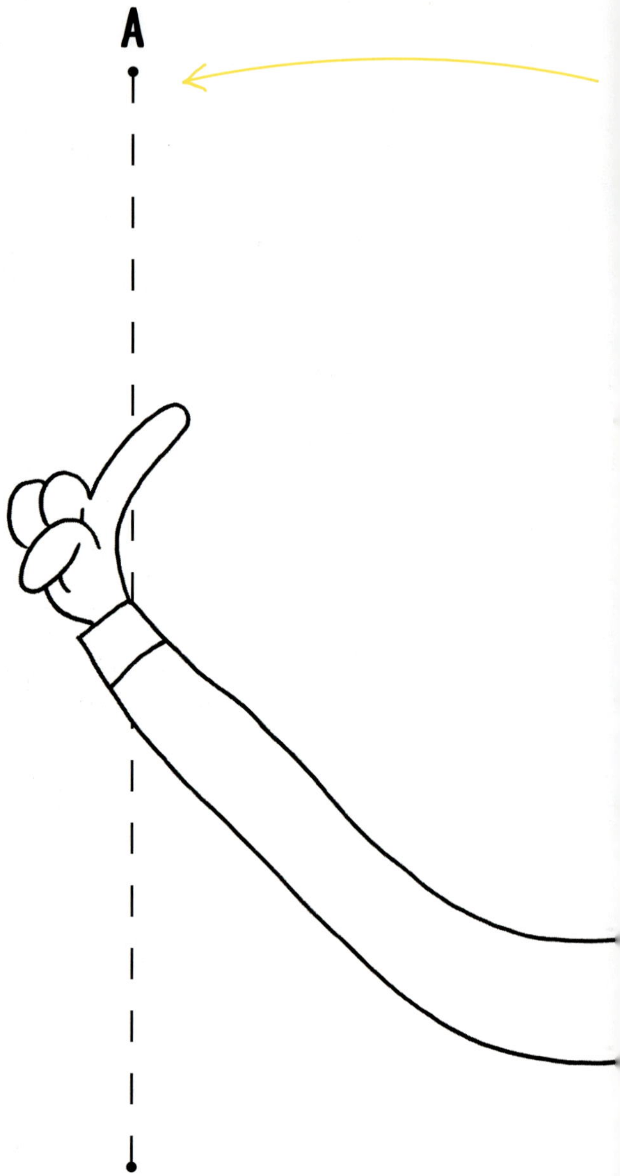
A

B
And again!
Mr Harris !

A

B

Fold line B over
to meet line A

Dad and Granddad were doing all sorts of

crazy

things with the

packing

tape!

But all that changed when Mum walked in and found us **laughing** . . .

Mum laughed, at first . . . and then **sighed**.

'You guys,' she said, 'I'm glad we're having fun, but we're never going to get the **house sorted** like this.'

'It'll take us **YEARS**
to unpack and clean up the **mess**.'

Mum sat down in a big pile of **bubble wrap** and **packing foam**.

I felt a bit bad as I looked at Mum, who looked really tired.

She'd been working **very hard**. Probably harder than all of us.

Mother's Day was almost here – it was just a couple of days away. It would be the perfect chance to make Mum feel **REALLY** special, and to show her how much I cared.

But I didn't have

ANY

money for a

fancy present.

What could I do?

I would have asked Dad and Granddad for advice, but they were too busy trying to **break out** of the packing tape.

IIIIIIIP!
GRRR!

And then it **hit me!**

I'd see if I could make some extra pocket money for doing all the chores around the house!

The house would get cleaned up really fast, **PLUS** I'd have some money to buy Mum a **great present!**

And I knew just who could help me . . .

BELLA AND HENRY!

WHOOSH!

CHAPTER 2

Luckily Dad agreed to my plan! Bella and Henry were **REALLY** happy as well – they both wanted extra pocket money to buy something for their mums for Mother's Day too!

WE ALL NEED POCKET MONEY!

The next morning, Dad took Mum, Sally and Roger out for the day to get some **new things** for the house.

Bella and Henry came over early so that the three of us could get started on the big **clean-up**.

We had a **HUGE** list of chores.

CHORES

1. Wash dirty clothes
2. Vacuum
3. Clean dirty dishes
4. Mow lawns and tidy yard
5. Throw away old magazines and newspapers

Granddad was home to keep an eye on us . . .

. . . but he **fell asleep** before we'd even begun!

'OK,' I said, 'first on the list is the WASHING. Do either of you know anything about washing machines?'

We had a **HUGE** basket of dirty clothes, plus a **BIG** box of washing powder.

How hard could it be?

Bella and Henry helped me tip the clothes into the machine. Even Dad's **underpants**.

'How much washing powder do we need?' asked Bella.

I shrugged.

'I know,' said Henry. 'The more we put in, the cleaner the clothes will be!'

That sounded pretty smart to me! So we poured in the whole lot!

Then it was time to **turn on** the machine. We thought we'd better go for the **highest setting**.

DISGUSTINGLY FILTHY!

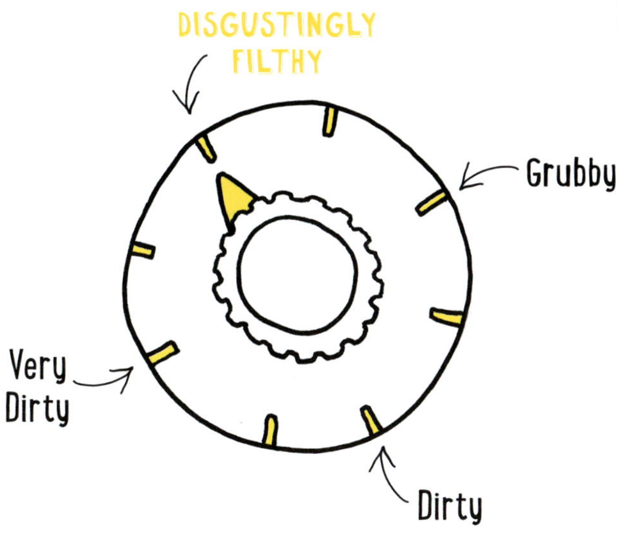

That should do it!

Next on our list was **VACUUMING!**

Henry grabbed the **vacuum cleaner**.

'I'm a lean, mean, sucking machine!' he said.

In moments, he was **zipping** around the house like a race car driver, while Bella and I watched!

It was **awesome!** All the dust and dirt was sucked out of sight!

Once he was done,
the **carpets**
looked like **new!**

But then Henry pressed some
weird button...

And all the dust and dirt **SPAT** right back out!

OOOPS. I GUESS I SHOULDN'T HAVE PRESSED THAT . . .

So . . . Henry started all over again!

But, this time, we made sure he didn't press that button again!

We moved to the kitchen next. We were ready to wash the piles and piles of dirty dishes that had built up over the last few days.

'That is **A LOT** of dishes,' said Henry.

'Sure is,' said Bella. '**Tiny** could take care of this in **seconds!**'

'And don't forget my dog **Mo!**' added Henry.

I didn't think Mum or Dad would like the idea of Tiny and Mo **licking** our plates **clean!**

'Here, guys,' I said, tossing them **gloves**, **detergent** and a **tea towel**.

Bubbles were flying

everywhere!

We made an awesome **washing**, **rinsing** and **drying** team!

And we only broke **ONE** plate!

MAYBE WE SHOULD
DRY THEM LIKE
THIS!

OR MAYBE NOT...

It took us AGES, but the dishes were finally done!

Bella took a deep breath. 'What's next?' she asked.

'Now we move to the YARD!' I said.

'Are we gardening?' said Henry. 'How about I just PLANT myself on the couch?'

Bella and I laughed.

A break would be great, but not just yet. There was still too much mess to clean up!

On our way outside, Henry stopped at our back door.

The back door had this cool round window. Henry jumped behind it and pretended he was underwater...

He couldn't miss a chance to make us **laugh!**

'Ha!' Granddad **laughed**, sitting up from his nap. 'I've woken up on a **boat!**'

Granddad had just woken up, right on time to help us out with the yard work!

He helped me get the

mower

going . . .

He helped Henry with the **whipper snipper** ...

And Bella with the **hedge shears** ...

We made gardening more fun by telling each other lots of **jokes!**

WHAT DO YOU CALL A COW THAT EATS YOUR GRASS?

A LAWN MOO-ER!

MOO.

HOW DO YOU MAKE A HEDGE TRIMMER?

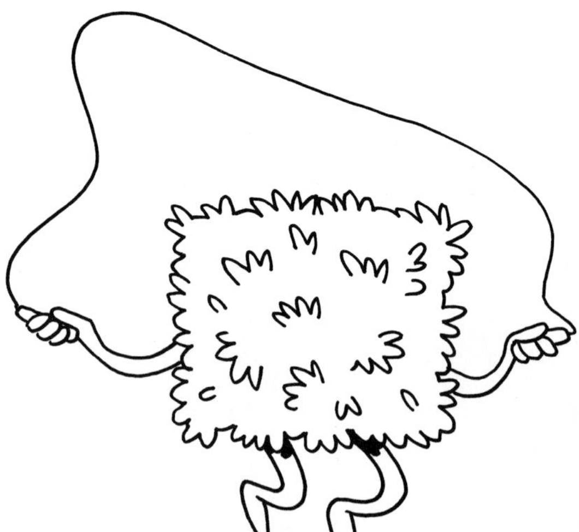

PUT IT ON A DIET!

WHAT TYPE OF **FISH** IS GOOD FOR CARRYING THINGS AROUND YOUR **BACKYARD?**

A WHEEL-**BARRA!**

After the long grass was gone, we discovered **HEAPS** of **cool things**.

Like a **bird bath**.

A fancy-looking **pond**.

A **slippery dip**.

And some **local wildlife!**

A **duck** …

A lizard ...

OOH, A BLUE-TONGUE LIZARD!
NAH, I'VE JUST BEEN EATING BLUEBERRIES.

A **frog** in the pond, listening to **music** . . .

CAN YOU GUESS
WHAT SORT?

HIP HOP,
OF COURSE!

And a **worm!**

The yard looked **INCREDIBLE!**

BEFORE.

AFTER!

But **WE** did not look so good!

Finally, it was **BREAK TIME!**

HUH?

CHAPTER 3

Granddad made us some sandwiches to eat up in the attic.

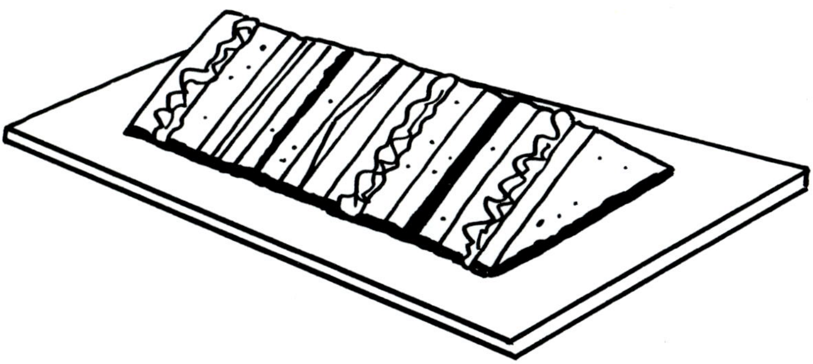

We had one more chore on our list.

5. Throw away
   old magazines
   and newspapers

But we really needed a rest first . . .

... and then we needed a JUMP around on the beanbags!

WHEEEEE!

They were so **bouncy** and **fun**.

WE TRIED

SOMERSAULTS,

BELLY FLOPS

AND
BACKFLIPS!

But we jumped around **SO MUCH** that the beanbags **BURST!**

We were sad about breaking the **beanbags** at first, but then we realised the attic had turned into a **really cool**

BALL PIT!

It was like **swimming** in a really cool pool,
without getting wet!

Bella and I were doing **backstroke** across the attic when I noticed something **weird** in the **corner** of the room.

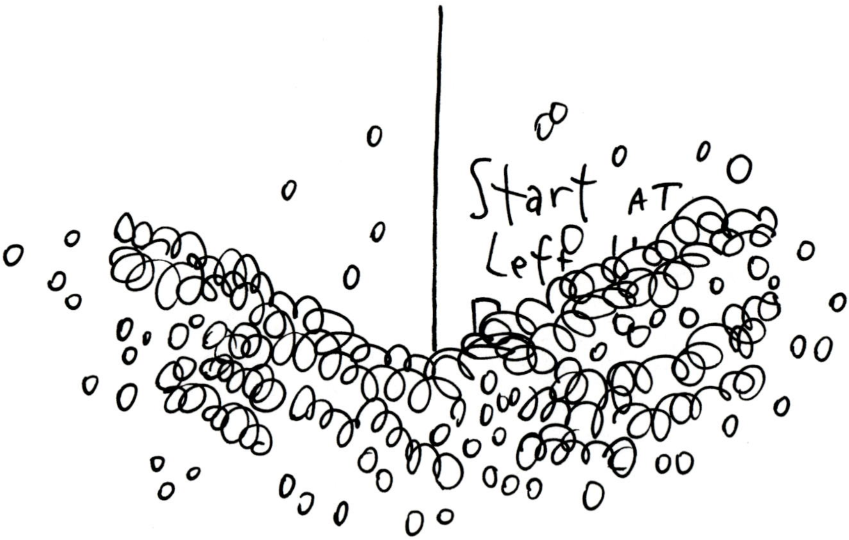

WHAT WAS THAT?

'Let's clean up so we can see properly,' said Bella.

It took ages, but we **packed up** the balls and then all three of us ducked down to read what was **carved** into the **wall**.

It was a bunch of **directions** and **numbers** ...

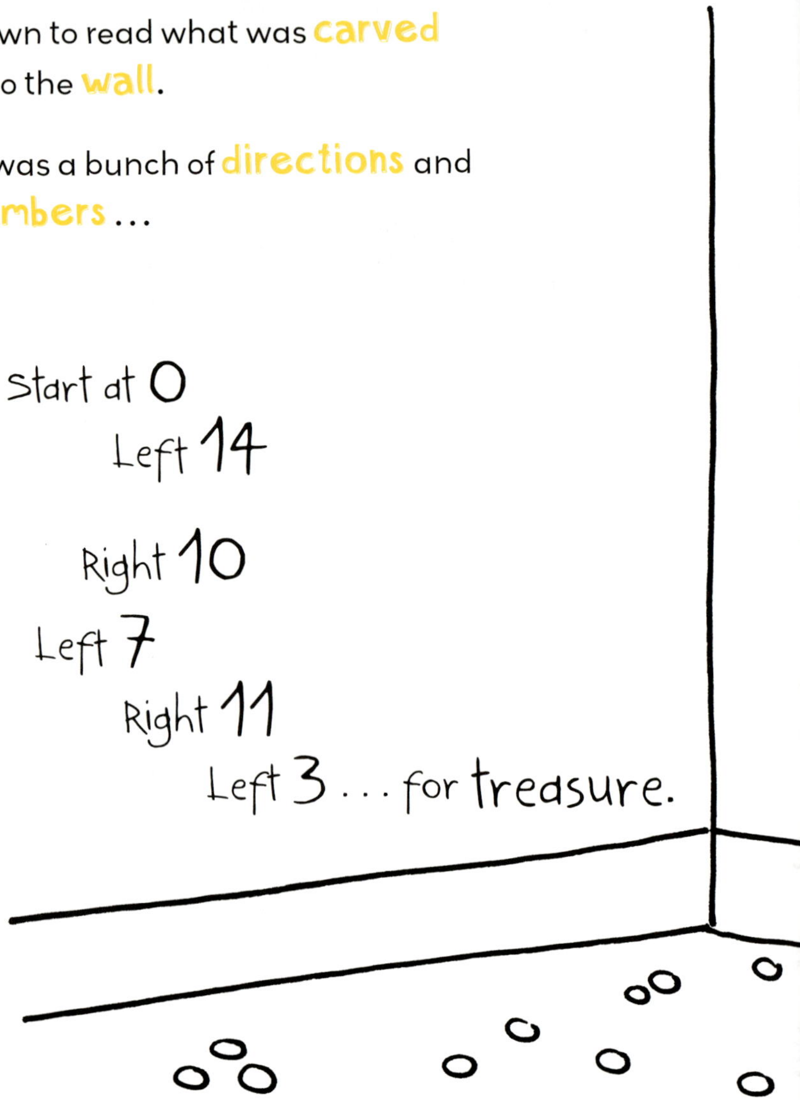

Huh?! *For* TREASURE?!

TREASURE!

This new house was about to get
a whole lot more interesting!

GURGLE!

CHAPTER 4

I kept thinking about that first instruction.
Start at O.

O? What could that mean?

Suddenly, I had a great idea!

'The back door!' I shouted.

'What about the back door?' said Bella.

'I think that's where we have to begin!' I said. 'The wall says to start at ZERO. That window looks like a big round zero! Maybe there's something buried in our BACKYARD!'

I scribbled down the notes from the wall, and we ran downstairs to start our treasure hunt!

'It must be **buried treasure!**' I said, as I ran. 'A pile of **gold** that some **pirate** left here years ago!'

Buried treasure would mean we could all buy **REALLY FANCY** presents for our mums!

We could send them on an incredible **island holiday!** They'd feel so **lucky!**

'What if it's a barrel filled with **REALLY** old coins?!' said Henry. 'They could be worth **MILLIONS! BILLIONS** even! We could buy our mums matching cars! They'd feel **SO SPECIAL!**'

OUR KIDS MAKE US FEEL SO SPECIAL!

'Or a chest filled with **diamonds** and **jewels!**'
said Bella. 'Our mums would be **so happy!**'

We skidded to a stop at the back door.

'OK,' I said.

I grabbed the shovels that were leaning up against the wall. I took one for myself and handed one each to Henry and Bella.

'Let's start here and take 14 steps to the left!'

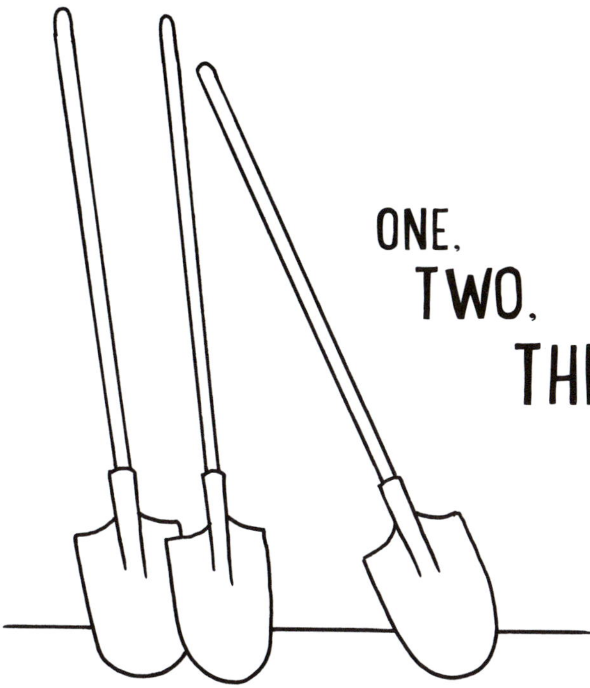

ONE,
TWO,
THREE...

Once we reached 14 steps, we turned and began counting 10 steps to the right.

. . . EIGHT,
NINE,
TEN!

Then there were another 7 steps to take to the left . . .

. . . FIVE,
SIX, SEVEN.

Eleven more steps to the right . . .

...NINE, TEN,

ELEVEN.

And lastly, **three** more steps to the left!

'We're here!' I said.

The three of us dug and dug

and dug . . .

. . . and dug

and dug

and dug . . .

‘Hey,’ said Bella. ‘What do you call a man whose head looks like a shovel?’

We'd dug really REALLY far, but hadn't come across any hidden treasure . . .

It was just dirt, dirt, dirt and more dirt!

We were about to call it quits when we heard this weird **bubbling noise** ...

Gurgle! Gurgle!

It was coming from the **house** ...

GURGLE!

GURGLE!

GURGLE!
UH-OH . . .

Suddenly, Granddad shouted from inside.

'THE HOUSE IS ABOUT TO *BLOW!*

WATCH OUT!'

And with that, there was a

HUGE EXPLOSION!

WHOOOOOOSH!
POP!
POP!
POP!

'Umm,' said Henry, 'maybe we **SHOULDN'T** have poured **all** of the powder in the washing machine . . .'

BUBBLES!

CHAPTER 5

It took us a LONG time to clean up after the washing machine explosion.

READY, SET, DIVE!

We removed buckets . . .

. . . and buckets . . .

of bubbles.

It was **slippery work!**

OOOPS!

But when we were done, everything looked **cleaner** and **sparklier** than ever!

'Super shiny!' said Bella. 'The house is looking **really** good.'

'So, Weir,' said Henry, 'what's left on our list of chores?'

I looked over at our list. We'd crossed almost everything off it.

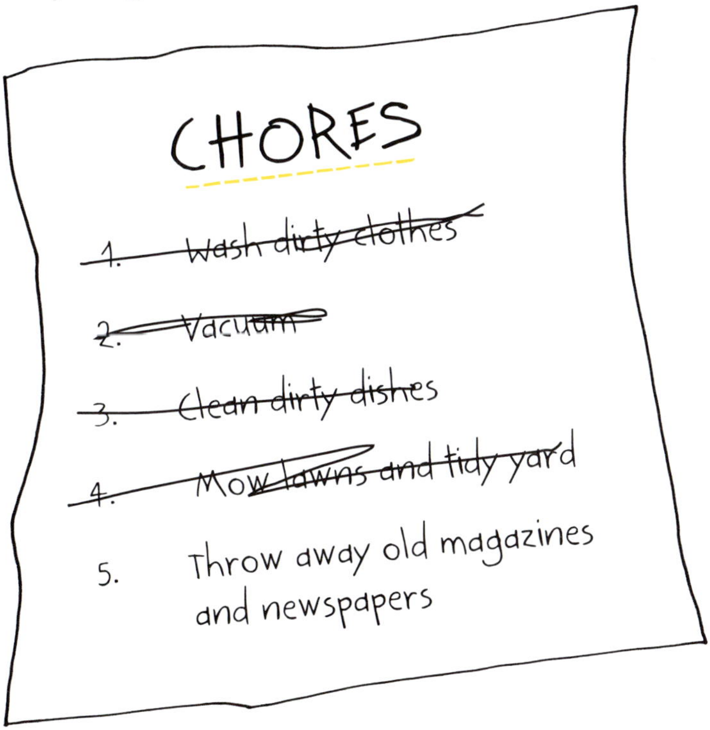

'We have to pick up all the old magazines and newspapers, then throw them in the recycling bin,' I said. 'And then we're done!'

I wished we'd been able to cross 'find buried treasure' off our list . . . and 'buy our mums awesome presents' . . .

But the **notes** on the wall had sent us on nothing but a **wild goose chase!**

CAN'T CATCH US!

We'd just have to use the **pocket money** we were earning today to buy our mums their **presents** . . . It wouldn't be as much, but it'd be something . . .

Granddad gave us some **empty boxes** to load everything into.

Slowly . . . but surely . . . we'd cleared up the mess! We were exhausted!

'You guys have REALLY earned this,' said Granddad, as he handed us our pocket money from Dad.

'Thanks!' the three of us said at the same time.

Now we could **finally** go and buy something for **Mother's Day** tomorrow!

We jumped into the car and Granddad **drove** us to the shops, but when we got there . . . it was **closed!**

NOOOO!

'It's too late!' I said. 'We spent so much time on the chores . . . the **shops** are already **closed!**'

'What are we going to do?' said Bella. 'I don't have **ANYTHING** to give to my mum . . .'

'Me neither,' said Henry. 'Maybe I'll have to write her a poem . . .'

I had **NO IDEA** what I could give my mum.

Sadly, we turned to drive back home.

But not before spotting Hans Some in the car park.

Back home, we **trudged** up to the attic.

We'd forgotten that it was completely **empty** now . . . there were no bean bags to fall onto.

But there was something **strange** in the corner.

'What's that?' I asked, pointing at the black box. We must have been so busy looking at the numbers on the wall earlier, that we didn't see it there!

Everyone rushed over to take a look.

'It's a safe,' said Granddad.

A SAFE?!

More importantly . . .

what was INSIDE the safe?!

CLINK!

CHAPTER 6

Granddad bent down and started pulling at the door.

He pulled and pulled . . . but the door wouldn't budge.

'It's stuck tighter than a superhero's underpants,' he said.

'Sorry kids. There's no way we can get this open without the **right code**...'

I rushed to grab the piece of paper I'd **scribbled** the wall numbers onto. Could this have been the **code** to the safe?!

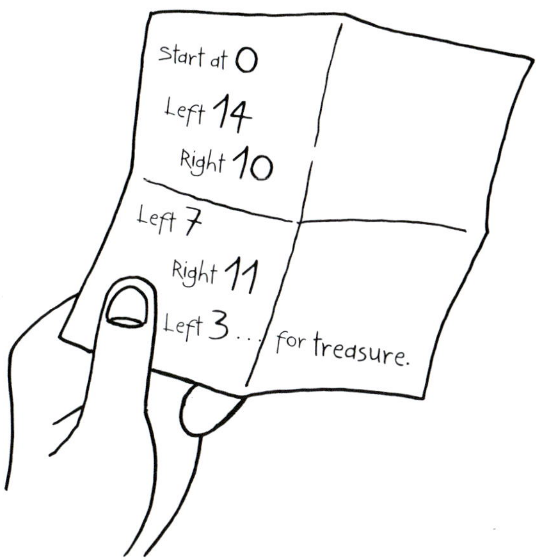

We were about to find out!

I knelt down in front of the safe. I turned the dial to 0, then followed the **instructions**.

Left 14 . . .

Right 10 . . .

I turned the dial **LEFT** for **7** clicks . . .

Right 11 . . .

Left for **3** clicks . . .

Then **CLINK!**

THE SAFE DOOR POPPED OPEN!
WHOA!

We'd done it! We'd opened the safe with the code from the wall!

Now **what was inside?!**

I reached in and felt around. In the back of the safe was a **small pouch**.

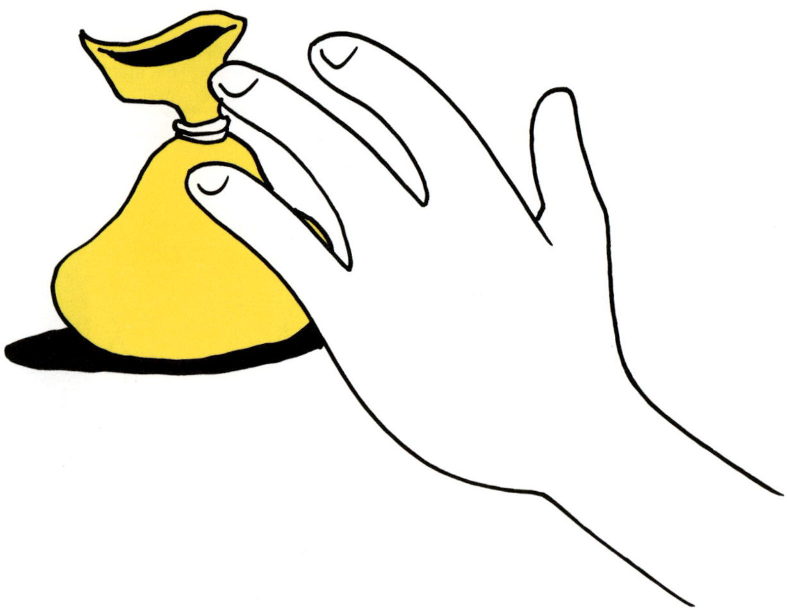

There was something inside!

I carefully tipped it out . . . and found three rings with blue jewels in my hand.

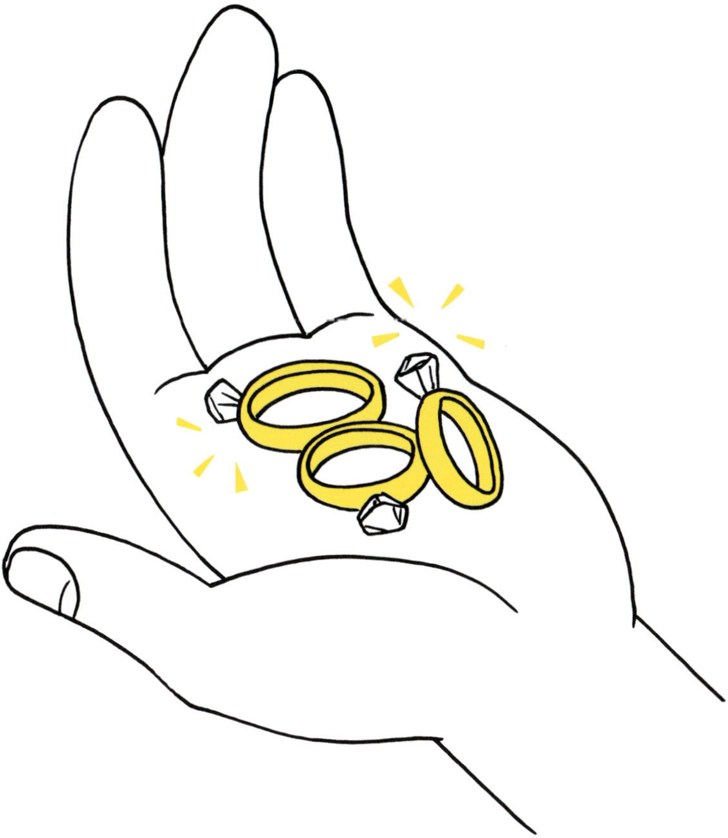

'Rings!' I cried out. 'We've found some **jewellery!** Jewellery we can give to our mums for **Mother's Day!**'

Granddad took the rings in his hands, then held them up to the light. He had a very close look at the gemstones, turning them over.

Henry and Bella and I watched on in **awe**.
We were so excited to have found something so **amazing** for our mums.

'Kids,' said Granddad, 'they're **beautiful** rings . . . but I'm afraid they're not worth a lot of money . . .'

OH . . .

Bella smiled. 'That's OK. They'll make great presents. You're the **Lord of the Rings**, Weir!'

MY PRECIOUS!

BEEP! BEEP!

The family was **home!** I quickly tucked the rings back in the **pouch**, and hid it in my **pocket**.

Mum and Dad were so impressed with how the house looked! Mum, especially, looked really happy . . . and, even better, really proud of us.

'Well done, all of you,' she added, giving Bella and Henry a hug too.

'Guess what we bought today?' said Dad.

'What? Tell us!' we replied.

'This!' said Dad, **wheeling** something **huge** through the front door.

A tree?!

'We'll need a very big hole to plant it in,' said Mum.

Bella, Henry and I looked at each other excitedly, thinking about the HUGE HOLE we'd already dug in the backyard today!

'We know the PERFECT spot for it,' I said, grinning at my friends.

BUMS!

CHAPTER 7

In the morning, we **planted** the new tree . . .

. . . and we set up a really long table for our big Mother's Day lunch.

We needed lots of space, because we'd invited Henry and Bella's families over to join us!

After **digging** for buried treasure and **cracking** the safe, we didn't find the riches we were hoping for.

We weren't going to send our mums away on **fancy holidays**, or buy them **new cars**, or spoil them with **expensive jewellery**.

But the rings were nice, and they were something we thought our mums would like. Even if they weren't worth a lot of money.

And we were right!

Our mums **LOVED** the rings . . . and all three of them put them on right away.

Henry ended up writing a **poem**, so he read that next. It was one he wrote for **ALL** of our mums!

Our mums . . .

We love you more than cookie crumbs.

When we're sick, you rub our tums.

When we were babies,
you wiped our bums.

Our mums . . .

We all cheered for Henry!

The mums also REALLY loved the sign we made for them . . . It was something we made last night out of some of the old newspapers and magazines . . .

Next, Bella, Henry and I took turns to say something **special** to our mums.

THANKS
FOR
MAKING ME
LAUGH
ALL THE TIME.

MUM,
YOU DESERVE
THE
BEST.

The three of them smiled. They looked very proud and very, very happy.

'We are the luckiest mums in the WORLD!' said my mum.

'Our kids make us feel so SPECIAL!' said Henry's mum.

'You kids make us so HAPPY!' added Bella's mum.

'Now let's eat!' Dad called out. He began dishing out all the amazing food he'd cooked us for lunch.

It was so good to see everyone eating and laughing and enjoying themselves.

WE LOVE YOU MUMS

I quickly **squeezed** into the seat next to my mum.

'I wish I could give you **all the treasure** in the world,' I said to her. 'But even that couldn't show you how much you mean to me.'

'Oh Weir,' she said. 'You kids . . . you, Sally and Roger . . . are the greatest treasures in the world.'

AUSTRALIAN BOOK INDUSTRY AWARDS WINNER!

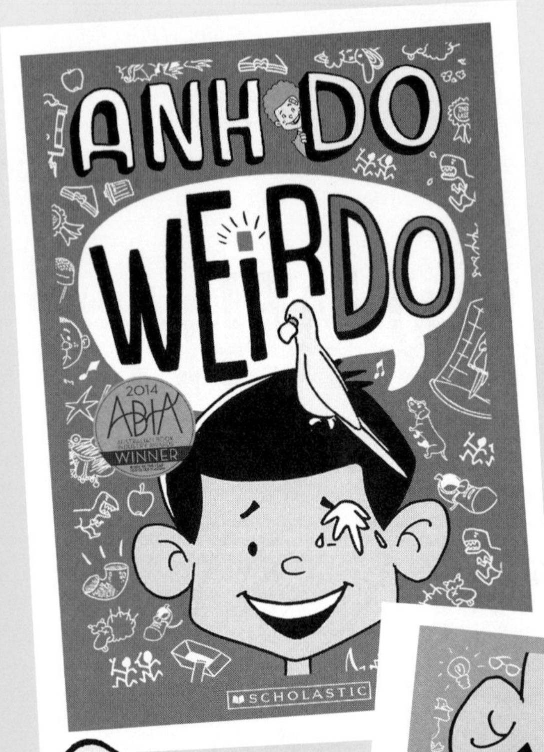

Book 1

GOT IT!

bird

Book 2

GOT IT!

COLLECT THEM ALL!

Book 3

GOT IT!

COLLECT THEM ALL!

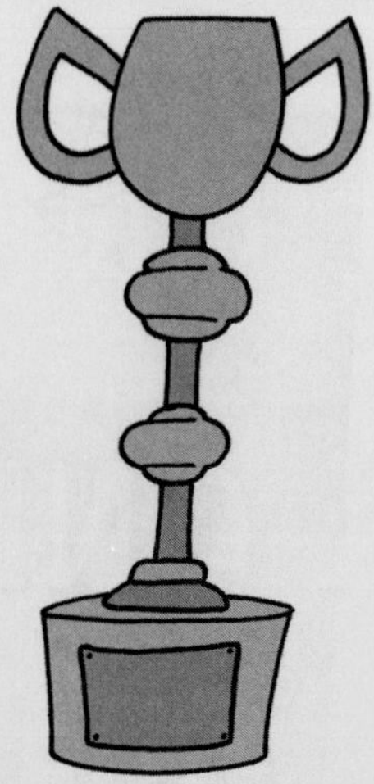

trophy

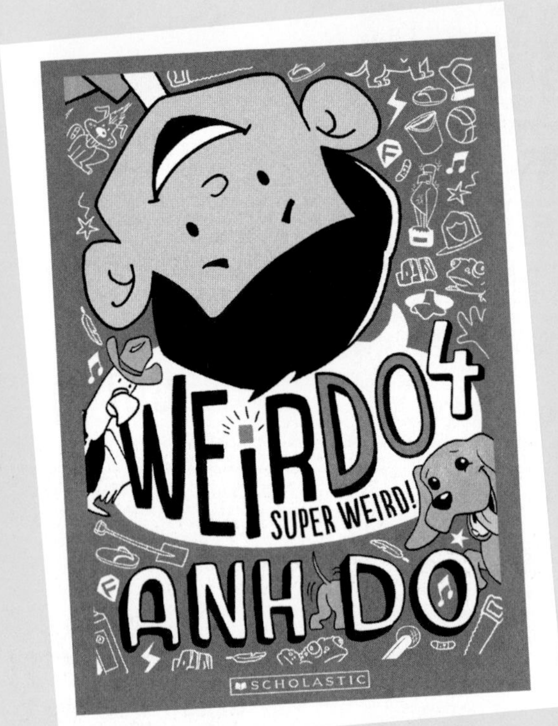

Book 4

GOT IT!

pet rock

pineapple

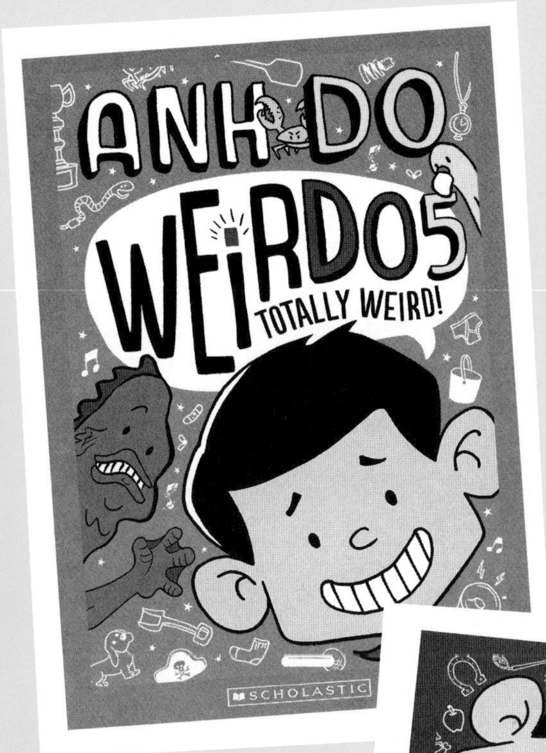

Book 5

GOT IT!

Book 6

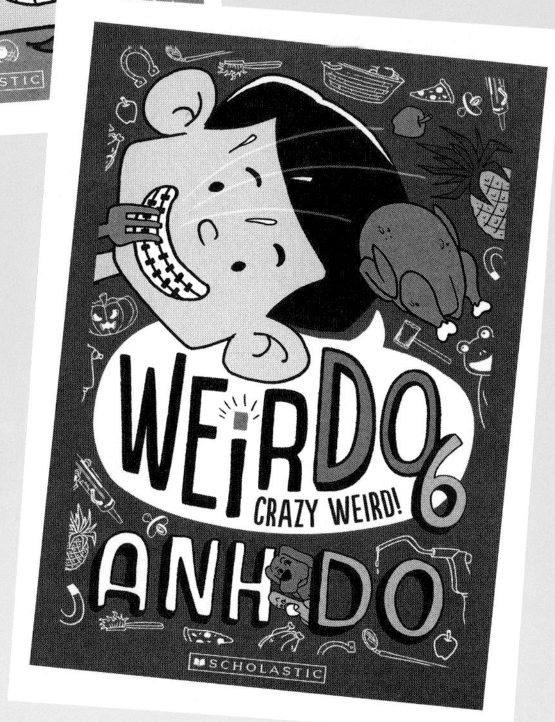

GOT IT!

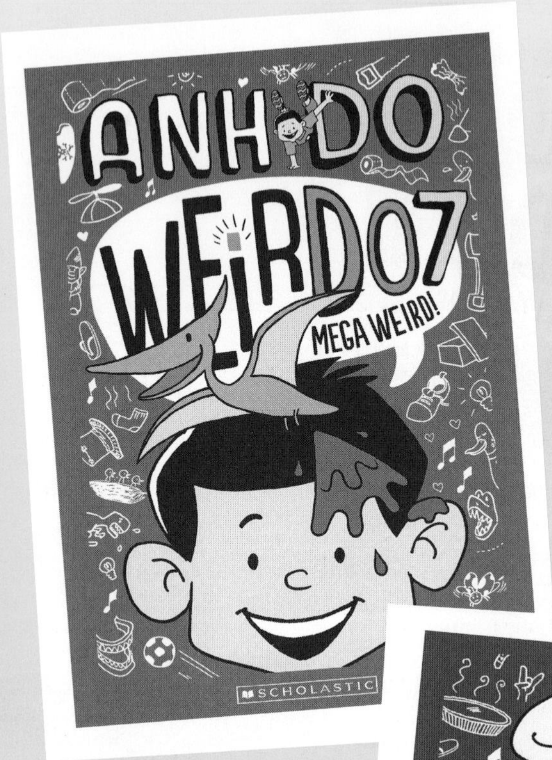

Book 7

GOT IT!

Book 8

GOT IT!

COLLECT THEM ALL!

Book 9

GOT IT!

YOU CAN NEVER HAVE TOO MANY WEIRDOS

barbecue

Book 10

GOT IT!

dirty dishes

worm

NEW
MEET NELSON THE NINJA KID!
ANH DO
NINJA KID
FROM NERD TO NINJA!
SCHOLASTIC
OUT NOW!

STAY TUNED!